Dan Nails It!

The End of Nail Biting

Written by: Vered Kaminsky

Illustrated by: Gali Korber

Dedicated to all children who are dealing with a nail biting habit. To Dan as well, who gave me his permission to tell his story.

∞

Thank you for choosing to read my book

"Dan Nails It - The End of Nail Biting!"

In order to add fun to the reading and understanding of the book, Dan's chart is waiting for you in PDF form, as well as the stickers and

the affirmations that helped him. Once you have read the book, post your email address in the link at the end of the book, and we will send you the chart and the other materials.

∞

Dan had been biting his nails for as long as he could remember.

It began at nighttime with his mother saying goodnight to him and turning off the light; he felt alone in his big, dark room.

As he grew older and he felt a little nervous or agitated, like at the beginning of the school year, his nails would always make their way into his mouth.

In the beginning, Dan's thumbnail was his favorite to chew. However, once he was finished chewing that nail and there was nothing left of it, he would move onto the rest of his fingernails. Slowly but surely, he would bite another fingernail, or even two. By the time he was 9-years old, every single fingernail of his had been completely bitten off.

By the time Dan was 10-years old, he excelled at sports and was the fastest runner at school.

He ran so fast that no one could catch up to him in running competitions. He made an effort to practice every single day, and he improved all the time.

However, the only thing he could not train himself to do was to stop biting his nails. His nails were very, very thin and tiny, with the skin around them peeling off and sometimes even causing sores.

Whenever his parents scolded him, he would stop biting his nails and would slide his hands into his pockets.

However, his parents were not around all the time, and when they were, they did not want to scold him all the time. They tried to make Dan realize that it was in his control to stop, but nothing actually did the trick.

If Dan was anxious about not studying enough for an upcoming exam and was afraid he would fail, or if he was worried about anything, his fingernails would pay the price.

When Dan was concentrating on something, or when he was lying in front of the television, or even after a long running practice, he would nibble his nails without even realizing it.

Biting on his fingernails provided Dan with some kind of comfort; it soothed him when he felt anxious before a running competition or before meeting with friends. It seemed to provide him with a feeling of control.

Fingernail after fingernail would be bitten - until there was nothing left.

In the summer, Dan used to hide his hands in his pockets all the time, so that no one could see them. In the winter, he would wear sleeves long enough to cover his hands.

Occasionally, by chance, if one of Dan's hands was visible and a classmate happened to get a look at his chewed fingernails, he would grimace and move away.

This would make Dan feel even more self-conscious, and resulted in him once again nibbling uncontrollably on his nails.

Some other children in Dan's class had bad habits as well.

There was Ron, who had the annoying habit of moving his leg uncontrollably when he sat down, which caused the table to shake. Maya's bad habit was to split the ends of her hair, which is what she did during every lesson. When she thought no one was looking, Glory would suck on her thumb.

However, Dan's nail biting habit was most often spoken about.

Dan felt self-conscious about trying to make new friends, so he withdrew more and more, causing him to nibble on his fingernails again.

Nothing Dan tried to do to help him break his habit was successful. He even covered his fingernails with a very bitter ointment. However, he managed to overcome the bad taste, even getting used to it.

He put gloves on, but managed to make holes in them to get to his nails.

He asked his mother to let him know whenever she saw his fingers in his mouth, but that did not work out well either. Sometimes Dan would get angry with his mother, but he did take his fingers out his mouth. However, as soon as his mother was not looking, he would nibble on his nails again. Eventually, both of them gave up.

One day Dan realized that his habit was a vicious circle that he was not able to break. He did not want to bite his nails, yet it provided him comfort and soothed him.

Feeling disappointed and discouraged with himself, he turned to his mother for help.

He asked her to help prevent him from biting his nails whenever he was under pressure or nervous or self-conscious, etc.

Dan's mother knew that the first step to helping Dan break his habit was for him to really want it himself.

"First, in order for you to stop biting your fingernails, you have to really, really want to break the habit, and then we can start to build a plan. When you really, truly want to, let me know!" she told Dan, walking away.

Dan sat and thought about what his mother had said. He thought hard and started biting on his fingernails without even realizing it. All of a sudden, he saw his image reflected in the mirror in front of him and, at that moment, he bit off too much of his nail, causing him to cry out in pain. His mother came into his room to see what had happened.

Dan said, "I have made up my mind. I want to get rid of this bad habit of mine. I want to. I really want to!"

And so together, Dan and his mother decided on a special plan to help Dan break his nail biting habit.

Dan's mother suggested, "We will divide the next two weeks into a plan of action, just as if you were training for a running competition. The first step is for you to define what your goal is and write it down."

"Ok, well my goal is simple – I want to stop biting my fingernails," Dan explained to his mother, and she grinned. Seeing her grin, Dan added, "Ok, well maybe it's not so simple, but I can do it."

After thinking a moment, Dan's mother got up and went to another room. She returned with a notebook in her hand and explained, "Here is a special notebook I prepared in advance, to help you to decide your plan of action on how to break your nail biting habit and then follow-up on the process.
This method is something I learned about, and it is great to have in your toolbox to achieve any goal you want." Dan's mother continued with a smile, "I knew that the day would come when you would want to break your nail biting habit. I wanted to be prepared to help you with it. On the first page, you will take your first step – which is defining your goal." When Dan opened the notebook, he saw a list of questions his mother had written down.

"Do not skip any question," his mother continued.

Dan looked over the questions and began to panic. He started feeling anxious and immediately one of his fingers made its way to his mouth.

When Dan's mother realized his distress, she said, "Take as much time as you need. When you finish this page, I will give you instructions for your next step."

Once Dan started looking over the questions, he realized that they were not as difficult as he had thought, so he began to answer them carefully, one after another. He completed the page and gave it to his mother. Together they read it over.

"Now that your goals have become clearer to you, you can start working towards them," she said.

Once Dan's goals were clearer, the next steps became easier. Dan's mother showed him the next page, which was a page she had called *The Value Page*. She said, "Values guide us like a compass to make choices based on what is important to us. Values such as friendship, learning, self-discipline, independence and creativity, give meaning to our lives and serve as goals for improving ourselves and making sure we never give up, until we have achieved these values. Living according to our values makes us feel truly fulfilled."

"Which values need to be pointed out to help guide you in breaking your nail biting habit?
Circle the values that you think will help you break your nail biting habit," Dan's mother instructed.
Dan circled the following values: *happiness, success, effort, self-confidence, pleasure, maturity, self-awareness, discipline, responsibility, humor and hope.*

Dan finished choosing his values and moved on to the next stage, which his mother explained to him just as he was about to go for a practice run.

She said to him, "Imagine there is a movie called *'Dan's New Life'*. This movie is all about you and your life, once you have begun the steps to break your habit. Begin with the first step you wrote down in your notebook and imagine moving forward, one step at a time, until you have finally succeeded and have reached your goal! What will your life look like once you get there? What will you be doing differently? How will you feel about yourself? What will you be able to do once you have broken the habit of nail biting? What will other people say about you? Imagine you are able to help others break their bad habits by telling them all about your success story!"

By the time Dan had finished his running practice, he knew exactly what kind of movie he wanted to make about the process he was about to go through, and he eagerly told his mother about it. Suddenly, his mother looked serious and said, "Dan, you need to watch out for the elf hidden inside your mind!" "What?" Dan asked. "What elf are you talking about?"

So his mother explained, "There is a small, but powerful elf hidden in your mind. It is hidden in everyone's mind! This elf tries to control you and will try to convince you that you will not succeed. The elf might seem sweet and harmless, but you need to be careful! He only wants you to listen to him and do what he says!"

"This nail biting elf could say: It is nice to bite your nails, so don't listen to anyone. You are not doing anyone any harm, so why stop? But, hey, guess what?" Dan's mother continued, "You can actually control your elf!"

"How?" Dan asked.

"By listening carefully when the elf speaks. You need to recognize that the elf wants you to fail, because he wants things to stay as they are, so you need to answer your elf, and that will help control it." Dan's mother could see that Dan was becoming agitated and upset about the elf, and that his earlier enthusiasm about the whole process was disappearing, so she decided to give him another idea on how to control the elf.

"Sit down and think about how you will feel once you have succeeded in controlling your elf," she suggested to Dan, and so he did.

Even though Dan was weary about the elf and afraid that the elf would "wake up" and disturb his habit-breaking process, he continued with the process.

Everything was going well until, as his mother had warned him, the elf popped up in Dan's mind to try to convince him that he did not really need to stop biting his nails.

The elf told him that it calms Dan and comforts him, and makes him feel better. This got Dan thinking why he should actually stop this habit, if it makes him feel good and comforts him.

Dan told his mother about his thoughts and doubts and she said, "It is time now for *affirmations*."

"What are *affirmations*?" Dan asked.

"*Affirmations are* positive sentences that you say to yourself over and over, to help you control the habit, and make you see the positive side of breaking your habit. So let's sit down together and think about what affirmations will help you and write them down on cards."

So Dan began writing *affirmations*, that he thought could help him look at the positive side of stopping his nail biting habit.

I am strong. I am smart enough to handle anything. I am creative. I believe in myself. I know how to ask for help if I need it. I know my abilities and I keep improving them. I use my sense of humor. I know that the ball is in my court. I will never give up!

Each time the elf "woke up" and tried to persuade Dan to give up, Dan would pull one of his *affirmation* cards from his pocket, and repeat it out loud. His favorite *affirmation* was:

I will never give up!

I believe in myself!
I am smart enough to handle anything!
I know how to ask for help if I need it!
I am strong!
I am creative!
I know my abillities and I keep improving them!
I use my sense of humor!
I NEVER give up!!!

Dan finished all the preparations to begin the actual habit-breaking process, feeling a little sad that he was going to have to stop the nail biting he was so used to. Yet he felt happy as well, that he was on his way to breaking his habit and stopping to bite his nails forever. Dan's mother then showed him a chart on which she had drawn a table divided into the days of the week.

She also showed him stickers with different facial expressions. Handing them both to Dan, she said, "Stick a smiley face on each day that you get through without biting your nails. Stick a half smiley face on days that you bite your nails a little, and on the days when you find yourself biting your nails often, you can stick a thinking face sticker."

Dan's Chart
Monday
Tuesday
Thursday
Friday
Saturday
Sunday

"When you feel that you need some help and encouragement, read over the exercises and your affirmations, and imagine the movie you made up for yourself. Good luck, Dan! I know that you will succeed!" his mother exclaimed.

Dan took the chart and stuck it on his bedroom wall. On the days when he managed not to bite his nails at all, he stuck a smiley face sticker on the chart; on the days when he found himself biting his nails occasionally, he stuck a half-smiling sticker; and on the days when he bit his nails often, he put a sticker showing a thinking face. It was not easy. In the beginning, the table was filled with all the different kinds of stickers. Dan found it very difficult not to bite his nails, and at some point, he even felt like giving up.

Dan's Chart
Sunday
Friday
Saturday
Wednesday
Thursday
Monday
Tuesday

Soon Dan came up with a good idea.

He drew a red smiley face on each of his fingers and every time he brought any of them to his mouth, he realized that the smiley face would become smudged and would dirty his mouth, and that helped him to refrain from biting his nails. Slowly but surely, there was only one kind of sticker that took over his board, and that was the smiley face sticker. After a while, Dan's fingernails started to grow back, and the skin around them improved. The most important thing was that Dan's hands were set free!

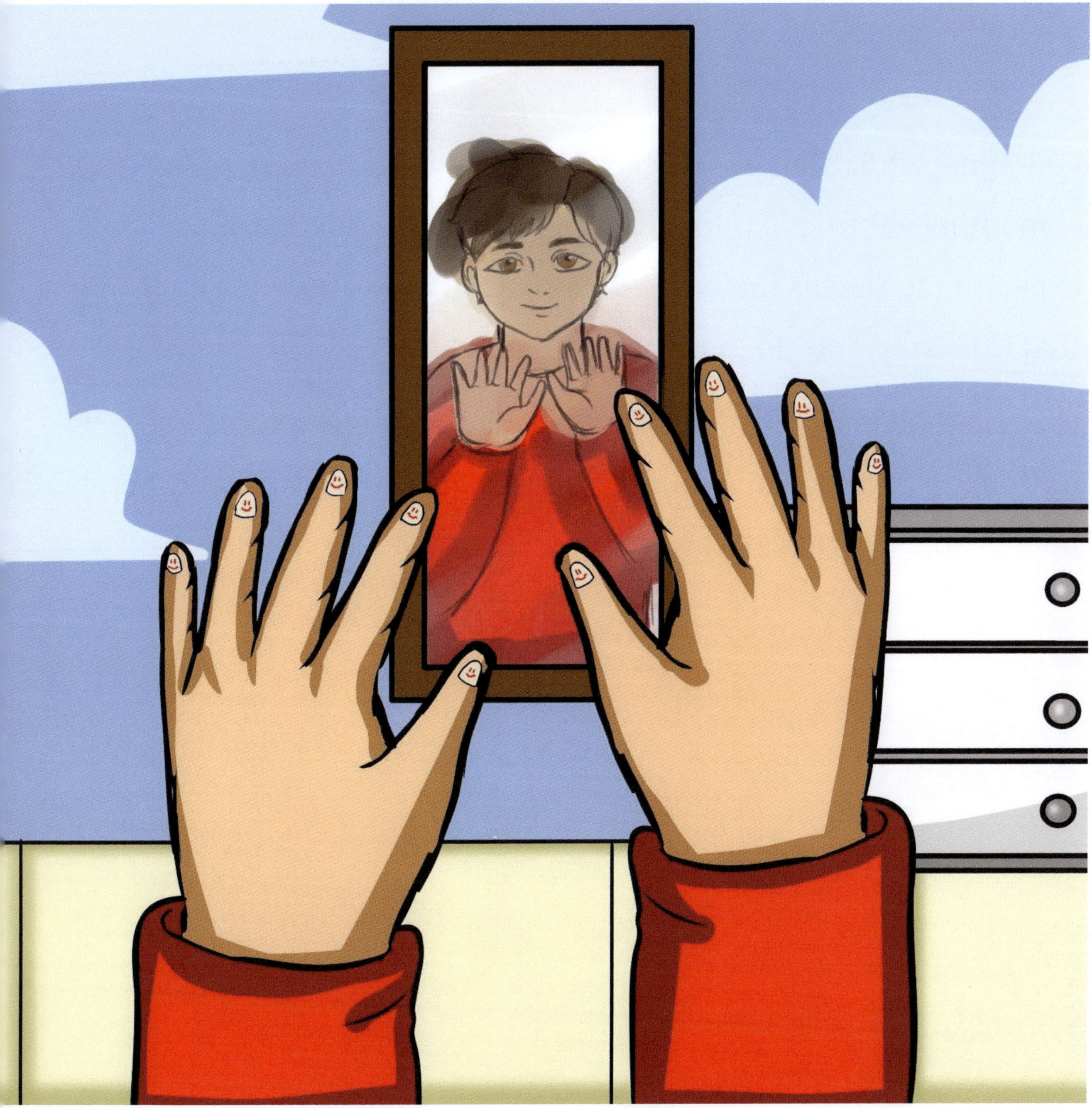

One time, while Dan was in class and one of his classmates said something about nail biting, they all turned to look at Dan, expecting to see his fingers in his mouth. Dan wanted to shout out that this habit was no longer a problem of his.

However, he just smiled at them, because he knew that he had nothing to prove to anyone. He had already proven to himself that he was able to break his bad habit and reach his goal!

If you can dream it, you can do it.
(Walt Disney)

Hi, I Hope that you liked the book and found it helpful.

You can find the chart, stickers and the affirmations in the link below:

https://bit.ly/2ZKYzdC

Good Luck!

Yours,

Dan

EPOS
DIGITAL PUBLISHER

Rights:
Vered Kaminsky
Epos Digital Publisher

© All rights reserved Printed in Israel, 2020

No part of this publication may be reproduced in any form whatsoever, including photocopying, scanning, recording, distribution of this book, or part of it, without obtaining prior written permission from the author.

Printed in Great Britain
by Amazon